I. Introduction

Supermarkets' pricing behavior differs across goods, and over time for many individual goods. Recent empirical studies of retailing behavior have revealed several regularities in retail pricing behavior. First, most retail price changes reflect changes in retail margins, rather than changes in wholesale prices (see Levy et al. [1999]). Second, most price reductions tend to be short-lived (Warner and Barsky [1995], Hosken and Reiffen [1999], Pesendorfer [1997]). Together these findings conform with the casual observation that sales, in the sense of temporary reductions in retail prices that are unrelated to costs, are an important aspect of retailer pricing behavior. Third, sales across various items within a supermarket are substitutes (Levy et al., Hosken and Reiffen) in the following sense. Supermarkets apparently decide to place a group of products on sale each week, and the identity of the specific items to be placed on sale is of somewhat secondary importance. Fourth, the magnitude and frequency of sales differs across types of goods (Lach and Tsiddon [1996], Hosken and Reiffen).

There is existing theoretical research on sales that provides an explanation for some of these pricing patterns. One explanation found in this literature is that sales are a means to intertemporally price discriminate for goods that either are infrequently purchased, or that can be inventoried by consumers (e.g. Sobel [1984]). An alternative explanation is that sales result from retail competition because consumers are heterogenous with respect to store loyalty (e.g. Varian [1980]). Hosken and Reiffen linked these two models to show how multi-product retailers, e.g. grocery stores, behave when they sell multiple goods. One implication of their work is that there should be systematic differences in pricing dynamics among goods based on consumers' costs of inventorying the good.

The goal of this paper is to provide additional empirical evidence regarding empirical regularities in pricing dynamics. The evidence extends previous empirical work and examines some of the predictions of the theoretical work. Our primary data source is a non-public use data set provided to us by the Bureau of Labor Statistics (BLS). This data set consists of 350,097 monthly price quotes on twenty different food items collected from retailers in thirty different metropolitan areas from 1988-1997. A key advantage of using this data set in studying sales is that we can observe a time series of

1

prices on a particular grocery item (e.g. z ounce container of brand x's creamy peanut butter from retailer y) for up to 5 years. Thus, we can examine how often different types of grocery products experience sales.

We establish a number of interesting facts about retail prices in the U.S. First, most products appear to have a "regular price." Using the BLS data, we find that for the 20 categories of products in our sample, products are priced at exactly their annual modal price 62% of the time. Moreover, in every category, products are priced at their annual mode at least 40% of the time. Consistent with Hosken and Reiffen, we also find that when prices are not at their modes, they are overwhelmingly more likely to be below the mode than above it. Second, products appear to go on sale more often when consumer demand is *high* (e.g., eggs before Easter). This is a somewhat surprising phenomenon in that most economists would assume that, other things equal, consumer prices would *increase* during periods of high demand. Third, it appears to be the case that there is substantial heterogeneity regarding which products within a category go on sale; i.e. in each category, certain brands and sizes are far more likely to go on sale than others.

We further explore this last finding using publically-available data provided by A.C. Nielsen, Inc. The advantage of this data is that we can obtain more detailed information on each particular item in the data set than we could using the BLS data. We focus on relating a product's market share (within a category) to the probability a retailer puts it on sale. We find definitive empirical results: for each of the seven categories of goods we analyze in two geographic areas, products with higher market shares are more likely to go on sale, and in all but one case, this result is statistically significant at conventional levels.

II. Theoretical Treatments of Retailer Behavior

This paper examines patterns in the pricing behavior of supermarkets. An important feature of this industry is that each firm sells a large number of individual products and the typical consumer purchases many individual products in each visit to a supermarket. Casual empiricism suggests that the pricing policies adopted by these firms differs across goods and varies over time for each good.

Specifically, a typical pattern is for a group of products to be put on sale by supermarkets (and advertised as such) each week, with the products in the advertised group changing from week to week.

The literature on price promotion by a multi-product retailer tends to focus on the information value of the advertising. A contribution which is particularly relevant in the supermarket context is the work of Lal and Matutes ([1989] and [1994]), who model competition between multi-product retailers located at either end of a Hotelling line, with consumers uniformly distributed along the line. They show that in equilibrium, competition between retailers results in prices which yield consumer surplus to all consumers.[2] The equilibrium level of surplus reflects consumer's costs of traveling between retailers.

Their 1994 paper considers the question of how that surplus is obtained; i.e., whether prices are set so that consumers obtain roughly equal amounts of surplus on all of products they buy, or whether some prices are set "low", so that the surplus is primarily derived from relatively few products. In the model, advertising conveys price information to consumers, and consumers (correctly) believe that any product whose price is not explicitly advertised will yield zero surplus (i.e., retailers charge consumers' their reservation value (H) for all non-advertised products). Based on this expectation and the prices of the advertised goods, a consumer will buy from the retailer whose prices yield the most greatest consumer surplus net of the transportation cost of reaching the retailer, as long as the net consumer surplus is positive. In equilibrium, the number of products each retailer chooses to advertise reflects a trade-off between two effects. Given that there is a cost for advertising each good, a retailer's advertising costs of guaranteeing any particular level of consumer surplus will be minimized by advertising a low price on a single product (with the expectation that prices will be equal to H on the remaining goods). Such a strategy may not constitute an equilibrium, however. If retailer i offers a price of (H - x) on a single good (charging H for all other goods), retailer j may find it profitable to offer two *other* goods at a price of (H - x/2) each, so that the surplus to the median consumer from buying all goods at retailer j is the same as the surplus obtained by buying that bundle from retailer i. In this

---

[2]Because each consumers' demand for each product is completely inelastic in the model up to a reservation value, there is a one-to-one relationship between consumer surplus and retailer profit.

case, if transportation costs are sufficiently low, consumers will "cream skim", buying some items at each retailer. If consumers behave in this manner, such a strategy by retailer j will be profitable, because retailer j will be selling a larger number of goods at higher margins than retailer i. More generally, the "cream skimming" effect works in the opposite direction as the advertising cost effect, inducing retailers to spread the consumer surplus across multiple goods.

Lal and Matutes [1994] demonstrate in the two product/two firm case that the only equilibria are characterized by both retailers advertising the same good(s) at the same price(s). Any good not advertised will be sold at consumers' reservation value for the good. It follows that in equilibrium no consumer buys from both retailers. When advertising costs are relatively small, then there are three equilibria. In two of the equilibria, a single product is advertised and sold at a price below H (one equilibrium in which each good is advertised). In the third equilibrium, both goods are advertised, and both are sold at less than H. If advertising costs are somewhat higher, but not prohibitive (i.e., not greater than half of consumers' cost of traveling between retailers), the only equilibria feature a single product being advertised and sold at a price below H. They suggest that in a model with more than two goods, all equilibria would feature multiple goods being advertised if advertising costs are sufficiently low.

While Lal and Matutes' equilibria suggests that either (or both) of the two goods may have low prices, their model has no direct predictions for which products will be priced low or high. However, the logic of their analysis does suggest that more popular products will be put on sale more often.[3] Consider their two retailer case, but suppose each retailer sells more than two products and that two of these products, A and B, are substitutes (as made clear below). We assume that α% of all consumers have a reservation value of H for one unit of product A and β ($>\alpha$)% of consumers have a reservation value of H for one unit of product B. The remaining $(1-\alpha)$% consumers place a zero value on consuming A, and likewise $(1-\beta)$% place a zero value on consuming B. Since $\beta > \alpha$, product B is more popular than product A. Further, we assume that A and B are close substitutes, in the following

---

[3]Lal and Narasimhan [1996] also conjecture that more popular items will be featured in the retailer's advertisements.

4

sense: δ_k% (k = A,B) of those consumers that derive utility from product k view the products as perfect substitutes, and $(1-\delta_k)$% do not value j ($\neq$k) at all. In addition, the value a consumer places on product A and B are independent of whether they purchase any other good. We assume that α, β, δ_A, and δ_B are the same over the entire Hotelling line.

Within this framework, we would not expect to see a retailer advertise good A and not good B in the symmetric equilibrium. To see the why, consider the extreme case in which everyone who values A values B, but the converse is not true; i.e., δ_A=1, δ_B < 1. In that case, there cannot be a symmetric equilibrium in which A is advertised at a "low" price, but B is not advertised, and priced at H. The reason is that if retailer i deviates by switching the prices and advertising strategies for the two products (i.e., advertise B instead of A), all of the customers who would have would have bought their bundle of goods from retailer i will continue to do so (since their utility is the same from buying A or B). Hence retailer i will retain all of the customers it would have had in the proposed equilibrium. In addition, retailer i will attract customers who value product B but not product A. Therefore, for the same advertising expenditure, a strategy of advertising B instead of A will be a more efficient means of bringing customers to the store (see appendix for the formal proof).

This case is unrealistic, in that it is unclear why a retailer would stock product A at all. However, the intuition holds in the more realistic setting where some consumers like A but not B (δ_A<1 and δ_B<1). If a sale on A alone is profitable, then a sale on B alone is more profitable, since B attracts more customers and all customers have the same reservation value. In contrast to the extreme case of δ_A = 1, it may be profitable to have both A and B on sale. Given the retailer has product B on sale, the benefit of placing product A on sale is the incremental increase in store traffic that results, $\alpha(1-\delta_A)$. As A and B become more differentiated (δ_A, δ_B become smaller), the retailer will have a greater incentive to place product A on sale as well. Thus, other things equal, we would not expect to simultaneously see sales on products that are very close substitutes. Hence, the prediction of this analysis is that there should be considerable variation in the frequency of sales with a product category; e.g., relatively popular brands of peanut butter have a higher probability of being on sale than relatively unpopular brands. Further, one would not expect to see two brands of products that are very close substitutes, e.g. Skippy and Peter Pan peanut butter on sale at the same time.

The Lal and Matutes framework explains why a retailer advertises a group of goods, charges low prices for those goods, and also provides some insight into which goods will be advertised. However, because the model is static, it does not provide an explanation for why the goods chosen to be advertised changes weekly, nor provide any predictions for the dynamics of retail pricing.

The main dynamic phenomenon we wish to investigate are sales, defined as temporary reductions in retail price which are unrelated to cost changes.[4] Two kinds of explanations have been offered for the sales phenomenon. First, Conlisk et al. [1984] have suggested that sales can be used to price discriminate between consumers based on differences in demand elasticity and willingness to wait (which is analytically similar to differences in costs of inventorying). If these differences are correlated (low elasticity customers are also less willing to wait), a seller can price discriminate by making high-elasticity customers wait for low prices. Hence, *sales* arise because periodic price reductions lead to a large volume of purchases by high-elasticity customers, while allowing the seller to charge high prices most of the time to low-elasticity customers.[5]

Varian [1980] provides an alternative explanation for changes in price that are unrelated to cost changes. In Varian's model, competing retailers each have some customers that are loyal to their store (buying from their preferred retailer as long as that retailer's price is below the consumer's reservation price). In addition, there are customers that buy from whichever store offers the lowest price. Each retailer has a choice between charging a "high" price, and selling only to store-loyal customers, or

---

[4] Several other kinds of systematic price reductions have been documented. One pattern is that prices for goods with a "fashion" element often systematically decline over a fashion season (see, e.g., Pashigian (1988), Pashigian and Bowen (1991), Warner and Barsky (1995)).

[5] Lal and Matutes (1989) use a similar explanation for competing multi-product retailers using different (static) pricing strategies for their array of goods. In their model, each retailer has a low price on a different good, which causes low transportation cost consumers to buy at more than one store each period, but allows the retailers to charge high prices on some items to high transportation cost/high reservation value consumers. Banks and Moorthy (1999), show that coupons can be another way of offering low prices to low reservation price/low search cost customers, while maintaining high prices to high reservation price/high search cost consumers.

6

charging a "low" price and potentially selling to non-loyals as well. Varian shows that the only symmetric equilibrium features mixed strategies, where all retailers choose their price from a continuous distribution. Hence, price changes in each period, even though the basic cost and demand conditions do not.

Sobel [1984] combines these two elements in his explanation of sales. In his model, there are multiple retailers, and high-value consumers are not only willing to pay more for the good and are less willing to wait (as in Conlisk et al.), but they also are loyal to one retailer (as in Varian). The primary difference between this model and Conlisk et al. is that while low-value consumers are willing to wait for a low price, they will buy from whichever retailer offers that low price. Hence, an individual retailer may miss the opportunity to sell to the group of low-value/non-loyal consumers because these consumers may have purchased elsewhere. In the multiple retailer model, each retailer faces the same basic decision: Is it preferable to sell to the group of high value customers at a high price, or to cut his price and sell to both these customers and the accumulated low value/non-loyal consumers before a rival does? As the length of time since any retailer had a sale increases, the number of low-value consumers rises as well, and this later option becomes more attractive.

The basic characteristics of the equilibrium in Sobel's model resembles the Conlisk et al. equilibrium. Retailers charge a high price when the number of non-loyal customers is small, but as the number grows, it eventually becomes profitable to reduce price to attract non-loyal customers. The key difference between the monopoly and multiple retailer equilibria is that in the latter case, competing retailers will consider having a sale sooner than a monopolist.[6] Hence, sales occur more frequently (and at deeper discounts) when there are multiple retailers. Another difference is that there will are a range of "sale" prices in the Sobel model. Finally, one can extend the model to show that the difference between the monopoly and multiple retailer cases is a general one. That is, a reduction in the number of competing retailers reduces the frequency and depth of sales, but does not affect the non-sale price of

---

[6]More precisely, in contrast to the monopoly retailer, with competing retailers the probability that a sale may occur becomes positive as soon as the expected profit from selling to the accumulated low-value consumers at a low price equals the profit from selling to the loyal consumers at their reservation value.

any good.

Hosken and Reiffen [1999] extend the Sobel analysis by considering competition between multi-product retailers. They show that pricing dynamics will differ across goods sold by multi-product retailers; goods which consumers can readily inventory will be characterized by less-frequent, but larger sales than goods which are less readily inventoried. Their model also implies that competition between retailers leads to some goods being on sale in each period. Because any individual good will only be on sale infrequently, the identity of the goods sold at low prices changes from period to period. As such, this analysis complements the Lal and Matutes model by explaining why the items that are advertised change from week to week.

III. Recent Studies of Retail Pricing Dynamics

Several recent empirical studies have examined the dynamics of retail pricing behavior. These studies have uncovered a number of empirical regularities that are broadly consistent with the theoretical literature described in section II.[7]

Levy et al. [1999] present detailed information on the cost and frequency of retail price changes for five supermarket chains. They exploit the fact that one of the five is located in Connecticut, a state which requires that each unit (e.g., individual cans) of most products be stamped with a price. They estimate that this law more than doubles the cost of changing a product's price. This difference provides them with evidence on the effect of higher cost of changing prices on the frequency of price changes. According to Levy et al., on average there was a change in the retail price for nearly 16% of all of items sold in the non-Connecticut chains each week in 1991/92. In contrast, the chain in Connecticut changed price on about 6% of their items in the average week (the total number of items carried by the Connecticut supermarket was similar to the other four chains). In addition, they present

---

[7]One empirical regularity that we do not discuss concerns the use of markdowns. Markdowns differ from the sales in the sense used here in that markdowns refers to price reductions that are not reversed, but rather increase over the course of a fashion season. Pashigian [1988] and Pashigian and Bowen [1991] document this phenomenon for apparel, and show evidence that the extent of markdown is related to the demand uncertainty for the good. Warner and Barsky [1995] provide additional evidence of this pattern, as the only good in their sample that has a fashion element (sweaters) displays this markdown pattern.

data on a group of products at that chain which are exempt from the individual pricing law. They find that about 21% of these items had price changes in the average week. Hence, it appears that the law induces more frequent sales on products in the exempt group than would occur absent the law. This kind of substitution of price reductions across goods is consistent with existing theory (especially Lal and Matutes [1994]). They also address the question of whether observed changes in retail prices solely reflect wholesale price changes, or whether some of the changes are changes in retail margins. They find that retail prices changes are 2 ½ times more common than wholesale price changes, so that most retail price changes are actually margin changes.[8]

Pesendorfer [1997] and Hosken and Reiffen [1999] examine prices at individual stores for specific product groups. Pesendorfer studies ketchup prices and finds evidence of the *sale* phenomenon. Consistent with Sobel, Pesendorfer finds that the probability a store has a sale, and depth of the price reduction increases with the length of time since the most recent sale. In addition, he finds that the percentage of days that the price of a bottle of ketchup is at a given level increases with the price level. That is, price is usually at a "high" level, and then periodically declines to a lower level for a short period of time. Finally, consistent with the Conlisk et al. and Sobel models, he finds that the volume of purchases made during a sale is larger the longer the period since the previous sale, and on average is seven times as large as when the product is not on sale.

Hosken and Reiffen [1999] address a different set of predictions, those regarding pricing dynamics of multi-product retailers. They examine the pricing of two products, in order to test whether the frequency and depth of sale differ between goods based on inventorying costs. Consistent with the theory, they find evidence that the good with low inventorying cost (peanut butter) has less frequent, but deeper sales than the good with higher inventorying cost (margarine). They also find evidence that the probability of sales on the two items is negatively correlated, suggesting that a store can substitute

---

[8]Specifically, Levy et al. had information about wholesale price changes for one chain. They find that wholesale prices increased for about 3.5% of goods each week, and assuming wholesale price reductions and increases are equally common, this implies that wholesale price changed for slightly less than 7% of items in the average week. In contrast, more than 17% of items have retail price changes in the average week for this chain.

between goods when deciding how to offer surplus to consumers. In addition, they find that the correlation of a product's price across stores in an area is quite low, and often negative. They interpret this to imply that most retail price changes are not driven by wholesale price changes, since fixed retail margins combined with frequent wholesale price changes would imply a high correlation.

Warner and Barsky [1995] collect and analyze daily data on retail prices for 7 infrequently-purchased durable goods (such as televisions, drills, and cameras). They find that most price reductions are short-lived, fairly significant (between 8 and 25 percent) and followed by a return to pre-sale prices. This suggests that the sale phenomenon exists for multi-product retailers other than supermarkets.

Lach and Tsiddon [1996] use data from the Israeli Central Bureau of Statistics to analyze retail prices for products in two food categories - meat and wine. The data is sampled at monthly intervals for a group of specialty stores in 1978/79. Their primary interest was documenting the frequency with which retailers adjust prices for their goods. Despite the fact that overall inflation in Israel was nearly 4% per month for the period covered by the Lach and Tsiddon data, they find that meat retailers were adjusting their prices only every other month, and wine retailers were adjusting their price only every 4-5 months. One other difference between the pricing dynamics for the two types of goods is noteworthy; they find that real price reductions large enough to cause a fall in nominal price are significantly more likely for wine than meat, even though the lower frequency of price change for wine would imply the opposite. This is consistent with Hosken and Reiffen's prediction that goods that are readily inventoried (like wine) have larger price reductions, conditional on a sale occurring.

An earlier study analyzing toy pricing by general merchandise retailers provides additional evidence regarding sales. Steiner (1973) finds that these multiproduct retailers primarily advertise price reductions on toys in the month prior to Christmas, when demand for toys is greatest. Moreover, within this category, advertised sales were most common for the most popular items. As a consequence, retail margins were generally inversely related to a toy's popularity. This provides some evidence that popular items are most likely to be placed on sale.

Taken as a whole, these studies suggest that a large portion of the observed variation in retail prices is driven by changes in retail margins. As discussed above, the theoretical literature provides two potential explanations for why sales occur. First, firms could be playing a mixed strategy in prices (as in Varian). Second, firms could be using sales to intertemporally price discriminate between high and low value consumers (e.g. Conlisk et. al.). A theory based on the Varian model appears to provide the best explanation of why highly perishable products that are frequently consumed (e.g. milk and eggs) are placed on sale.[9] For easily storable non-perishable products (e.g. ketchup or canned tuna) or infrequently consumed perishable products (e.g. fresh salmon), either the price discrimination or mixed strategy in prices models could describe retail pricing behavior. However, some empirical evidence suggests that consumers "stock-up" during sale period, thus, the price discrimination model may be more appropriate in describing why firms offer sales on non-perishable items.[10] Section V provides some additional evidence regarding the prevalence of sales, and some evidence regarding the characteristics of those products that are put on sale by supermarkets. Section IV describes the data used.

IV. Data Description

This paper identifies and provides an explanation for some empirical regularities in retail price variation. We use two different data sets in our analysis. The first is a non-public use data set we obtained from the Bureau of Labor Statistics (BLS). To our knowledge, this data has not been used in previous academic studies. For this reason, we provide background information on this data source. In collecting the data used to calculate the Consumer Price Index, the BLS samples food retailers in 88 geographic areas, collecting prices of specific items in up to 94 categories of goods.[11] Within each

---

[9]Because these products cannot be readily stored, firms cannot intertemporally price discriminate against high and low valued consumers of these products

[10]For example, Pesendorfer (1997) finds that seven times as much ketchup is purchased in sale weeks than non-sale weeks.

[11]Where a category is a fairly narrow classification of consumer goods, e.g. cola drinks, eggs, and white bread are BLS categories.

category, the BLS samples the price of a specific item at the same store monthly for up to 5 years. That is, if in the first month, the BLS uses a 2-liter bottle of Pepsi as its cola product in a specific store, it will continue collecting pricing data on 2-liter bottles of Pepsi as a cola item as long as the store remains in the sample, and 2-liters bottles of Pepsi remain on the shelf at that store. The number of retailers sampled in each area increases with the area's population. In each geographic area the BLS changes all of the stores in its sample every five years. Hence, the largest potential number of observations in any individual price series is 60. The choice of which specific item(s) in a category to sample from each supermarket is based on a weighted-average randomization. For example, if Pepsi in the 2-liter bottle represents 10% of cola revenue in a supermarket, then the BLS randomization results in a 10% chance that 2-liter Pepsi will be the sampled cola product.

The data we use in this study consist of individual price series for specific products. For example, each price series in the cola category in Chicago contains observations on the price of a specific brand and container size of cola at a retail outlet in the Chicago area, each month for up to 60 consecutive months. Most product categories have multiple price series in each geographic area. Unfortunately, the price series provided to us do not contain information that identifies the specific product and package size sampled within each category. We only know that all of the prices within a price series correspond to prices for a specific product at a specific store within a category. We do not know is, for example, whether that specific cola product is a 12-pack of Coca-cola or a 2-liter bottle of Pepsi-cola.

The data we received from the BLS contains all of the price series the BLS collected on 20 categories of goods (cereal, white bread, cookies, crackers, ground beef, hotdogs, eggs, cheese, bananas, lettuce, frozen concentrated orange juice, margarine, peanut butter, cola drinks, canned soup, frozen dinners, snack foods, baby food, soap and detergents, and paper towels) from 30 geographic areas[12] for the period 1988-1997. Tables 1-4 provide some descriptive information about the data set.

---

[12]These areas are: Atlanta, Boston, Buffalo, Chicago, Cleveland, Dallas, Dayton, Denver, Detroit, El Paso, Greater Los Angeles, Jacksonville, Kansas City, Los Angeles, Miami, Minneapolis, New Orleans, New York and Connecticut suburbs of New York City, Philadelphia, Portland, Richmond, St. Louis, San Diego, San Francisco, Scranton, Seattle, Syracuse, Tampa, Tucson, and

Table 1 shows that the observations are fairly evenly distributed throughout the sample period, although some years do have more observations than others. Table 2 presents both the number of unique price series and number of observations for each product category. Our data contains far more information on some grocery products (e.g. ground beef and white bread) than others (e.g. baby food and paper products). This reflects a policy on the part of the BLS to collect more data on products that are viewed as more important in measuring the CPI. Table 3 shows the number of price series and items by geographic area. The sample contains much more information from larger population areas than smaller areas.

Table 4 presents a frequency distribution of the length of the individual price series separately for each product category. As discussed earlier, under the BLS sampling scheme, an individual price series can be as long as 5 years. However, as seen in Table 4, only a small fraction of price series in our sample attain a length of 5 years. In fact, the majority of price series are less than 2 years in length for all product categories except ground beef, eggs, orange juice, and lettuce. According to the BLS, there are two reasons why most of our price series have relatively short lengths.[13] The first reason is that we obtained the same ten calendar years (1988-97) of data for all cities. Because the BLS changes its sample of stores for 20% of its cities each year, 80% of the observations in the first year of our data are part of a series that began in a previous year. Hence, 80% of the observations for 1988 will be part of a time series that began outside of our sample period. Similarly, 80% of the observation for 1997 will be part of a time series that will conclude outside of our time period. This means that for the 80% of 1988 observations that are parts of prices series that began before 1988, the maximum series length will be 48 months, and for 60% of the observation the maximum series length will be 36 months, etc.

A second reason is that if the BLS surveyor arrives at the store and cannot find the exact product and package size of a particular item, she selects a new product in that category and creates a

---

Washington D.C.

[13]Some of the price series have lengths longer than 5 years because the BLS collected an additional year of data for the regions that were rotated out in 1997 for the update of the CPI.

13

new price series. In the data set, it appears this is the primary reason why most of the time series are so short. For some of the product categories, e.g. canned soup or frozen dinners, this explanation seems plausible. These product categories have many different individual brands and package sizes, and it seems reasonable to believe that the life span of a randomly selected product is short. However, for more stable categories, e.g. cola drinks, we find this explanation less credible. It is well known that there are two major brands of cola (Coke and Pepsi) that come in four different varieties (the permutations of with and without sugar and caffeine) that have been on the market with a commanding market share throughout the sample period. It seems unlikely to us that changes in the product mix would result in 40% of the price series for cola drinks being less than one year in length. The unexpectedly short duration of many of the individual price series appears to be the major shortcoming of the BLS data set. However, while the short length of some of our price series weakens our ability to detect price changes, it does not induce any bias into our analysis.

In order to examine sale behavior, we must operationalize the idea of a sale as a significant temporary reduction in the price of a retail item. We do this by saying that a sale occurs if a product's price falls by some fixed amount in a given period and then rises by a similar amount in the next time period.[14] In many ways, the BLS data is well-suited to measure sales. We typically observe the same product over a relatively long time period and can observe when it experiences a temporary reduction in price. Furthermore, because we have observations on many products for a large cross-section of U.S. cities, we feel confident that our results are robust.

Nevertheless, there are two significant weaknesses in using this data set to determine whether popular products go on sale. First, prices are sampled monthly, whereas previous research suggests that sales last either one or two weeks and the ideal frequency of observation would be weekly (See Hosken and Reiffen, [1999], Pesendorfer [1997]). In a large sample, this should not affect the proportion of our observations that are *sales*, but will reduce our ability to detect *sales*. The reason

---

[14]We have considered five different price decreases in our definition of sale - 5%, 10%, 15%, 20%, and 25%, although in the interest of brevity, only the results for the 10% and 20% definitions are presented here.

that sales are more difficult to observe is only partially due to the reduced number of observations. A more fundamental problem arising from having less-frequent observations is that the retailer's costs are more likely to change between observations than if the data were weekly. Thus, some of the price movements we detect may reflect wholesale price changes rather than sales. A second weakness is that, because we do not know the exact product and package size sampled, it is impossible to relate a product's characteristics, such as its market share, to the likelihood it goes on sale.

The second data set we use comes from a public use data set provided by A.C. Nielsen.[15] This data set contains daily product prices for seven categories of goods (peanut butter, tub margarine, stick margarine, tuna, ketchup, and facial tissue) at the individual store level for two medium-size cities in the mid-western U.S. (Springfield, MO and Sioux Falls, SD) for the 124 week period beginning January 23, 1985 through June 3, 1987. In addition, the data set contains market shares based on product revenues for each product category and city. There are five supermarket chains in Sioux Falls, and four chains in Springfield. An attractive feature of this data set is that the researcher knows daily product prices for each brand and package size within a product category (e.g. 18 ounce Peter Pan creamy peanut butter). Hence, using this data set we can directly relate a product's popularity (as measured by the its market share) to the likelihood a retailer puts the product on sale. The weakness of the data set is that in covers a relatively small set of products for a short time period in only two cities.

V. Empirical Findings

In this section we present some empirical evidence related to the predicted pricing dynamics described in Section II. One implication of the analysis in Section II that seems to have empirical support is that most products should have a predictable "regular price", and irregular downward deviations from that price. Another implication is that within each category, popular products should have more frequent sales.

To examine the question of whether products have a "regular price", we first calculate how often an individual product's price is at its "typical" level. Specifically, we conduct the following

---

[15]The data can be found at the ftp site: gsbper.uchicago.edu.

calculation: we first divide the data set into individual time series for each calender year (e.g. the tenth price series for peanut butter in Chicago for 1996). Next, for each annual time series, we calculate the modal price. We then calculate how often the store's price for the item was equal to the modal price. Finally, we compile frequency distributions describing how often the prices in each individual time series are equal to their modal values for each product category. Summary statistics from these frequency distributions are presented in table 5. With the exception of eggs and lettuce, the products' prices are equal to their modal value at least 50% of the time. Furthermore, with the exception of eggs, lettuce, and bananas more than 25% of products are at their modal prices at least *75%* of the time. Clearly, most products have a "regular" price. Another interesting observation from table 5 is the difference between goods based on inventory costs. Eggs, lettuce, and bananas are clearly the most difficult products in our sample for consumers to inventory, and are the least likely to be equal to their modal prices (consistent with the analysis in Section II).[16]

Having established that most products have a regular price, we next examine whether most of the variability in product prices is the result of relatively permanent changes in wholesale prices or the result of temporary decreases in product prices, i.e. sales. We address this question by calculating the percentage of deviations from the modal price that are above or below the mode for each type of product in our sample. If product prices only change as the result of permanent changes in wholesale prices, we would expect the percentage of prices above the mode to be about the same as the percentage of deviations below the mode.[17] Conversely, finding that when the price is not at its mode, it is generally below the mode suggests that price changes are driven by retailer behavior. As seen in Table 6, for every category, prices below the mode are much more likely to occur than prices above the mode. In each product category, the difference between the number of downward deviations from

---

[16]At the same time, lettuce, and to a lessor extent, bananas and eggs have more seasonality in wholesale prices than most of the other goods in our sample. Hence, some of the differences in the observed percentage of time at the mode are undoubtably due to differences in the variability of wholesale prices.

[17]Implicitly we assume there is no systematic pattern in wholesale price changes, e.g. manufacturers changing prices every March.

the mode is higher than the number of upward deviations by a statistically significant amount. Thus, the data suggests that sales are the leading cause of retail price variation for a wide variety of goods sold by retailers.

As discussed earlier, our extension of Lal and Matutes's [1994] theory suggests that popular products (defined as products consumed by a large proportion of consumers) should be the items placed on sale most frequently. An implication of this result is that products should systematically differ in their likelihood of going on sale. In particular, in a cross-sectional comparison one would expect to find that popular products should go on sale fairly frequently while unpopular products should go on sale less frequently. We propose to indirectly test this prediction as follows. If all products are equally likely to go on sale, then knowing whether a particular product went on sale in a given year should not help predict whether the product will go on sale in subsequent years. Thus, we wish to test the null hypothesis of whether the probability of observing a sale on a particular product in year t is independent of whether that product was on sale in year t-1. The alternative implied by the theory is that the probability of observing a sale in period t is higher for products which had a sale in period t-1.

To test this hypothesis we perform the following calculation. First, for the first twelve months of every price series in the data set, we record whether that price series experienced a sale.[18] Next, we divide the sample into two parts: The first contains price series that have a sale in the first twelve months and the second contains those price series that do not have a sale. Within each product category we then calculate two conditional probabilities; the probability that a price series would experience a sale during the second year of the sample (so that the probabilities are calculated only for series with at least 24 observations) conditional on the product being in the first group (i.e., having a sale within the first 12 months), and the probability of a sale in the second year conditional on being in the second group. We then test the null hypothesis that the conditional probability of observing a sale is the same for both

---

[18]Where a sale as defined as observing at least a certain percentage decrease in a product's price between month t-1 and t, followed by a the same percentage price increase from month t to t+1. Since there is no obvious definition of how large the relevant change has to be, we consider sales of 5%, 10%, 15%, 20%, and 25%. Only the 10% and 20% results are presented here, but the results are quite similar for other definitions, and are available from the authors upon request.

groups. The results appear in table 7. For *every* product category in our sample the conditional probability of observing a sale is larger, often substantially larger, if the price series experienced a sale within the first 12 months. In fact, in 38 of the 40 hypothesis tests listed there, we reject the null hypothesis with a z-statistic greater than 2.5.[19] For example, as panel a shows, of the 77 cereal price series that experienced a 10% sale within their first 12 months in the sample, 53.2% experienced at least one additional 10% sale in the second 12 months of the sample period, while only 29.2% of the 336 price series that did not experience a sale within the first 12 months experienced at least one 10% sale in the second 12 months. The difference in these conditional probabilities is significant at virtually any level of statistical significance (z=5.29). We interpret this as strong evidence that there is substantial heterogeneity across products in the likelihood of having a sale. Retailers appear to systematically place some products within a category on sale more often than others. This result is robust across 20 large categories of goods, over time, across the U.S. and for five different definitions of sales (5%, 15%, and 25%, as well as the 10% and 20% reported here). Unfortunately, using the BLS data it is not possible to relate which product characteristics (e.g. a product's market share) are associated with going on sale, however, the data does suggest that products differ widely in the frequency with which they are put on sale.

Thus far, the discussion has focused on the relative popularity of goods within a category (e.g. different types of peanut butter or bread). However, one would also expect that retailers would be more likely to have sales on categories of goods that are more popular. While it is difficult to determine which categories of goods are most popular with consumers,[20] we know some goods become more

---

[19]The corresponding number of z-statistics over 2.5 using all 5 sale definitions was 91 out of 100. Note that for some of the comparisons of conditional probabilities, the number of price series is very small. In these cases it is incorrect to assume that the difference in proportions is approximately normal, and instead we simply interpret the computed z-statistics as measures of the size of the difference between conditional probabilities.

[20]From existing data sources we have found, it is difficult to determine which categories of goods are most popular with consumers. For example, while we can find information on aggregate consumption of peanut butter, however, it is unclear what proportion of people consume peanut butter or given they consume peanut butter, how often they consume it.

popular at certain times in the year; that is, there is seasonal demand for certain products. Of the twenty products in our sample, we identify five which have predictable seasonal changes in demand. The demand for soup increases in the fall and winter (October thru March), peanut butter demand increases as part of back to school planning in August and September, egg demand increases around Easter, and ground beef and hot dog demand increases in the summer (June, July and August). Further, because the costs of producing these items are not seasonal, we are reasonably confident that any change in sale behavior is a result of retailers' reactions to changes in demand rather than supply. Thus, an additional test of the analysis is determining if sales on these products are more likely to occur in periods of high demand. The results of these tests are presented in table 8. Again, the results strongly support the theoretical analysis. We see for any of the sale definitions we consider, retailers are more likely to put these items on sale in periods of high demand, and that these differences are statistically significant in virtually all cases at any standard significance level. Thus, our data suggest that retailers systematically *lower* the prices of items which experience increases in demand. While these results are not surprising to anyone who shops in a grocery store, the analysis presented here provides an explanation for this phenomenon: A retailer attracts a consumer by offering more consumer surplus than its rival does. In order to inform consumers of the surplus that can be obtained, retailers invest resources in advertising sale prices. Thus, other things equal, retailers will choose to put items on sale that are attractive to the widest audience possible. Hence, when products have known upward spikes in demand, we would expect retailers would find it more attractive to put these items on sale.

Using the BLS data we have seen that products appear to have a regular price and that most deviations from that price appear to be sales. Further, we have seen that there is substantial heterogeneity across products in the likelihood a retailer puts a product on sale. Within each product category, e.g. peanut butter, some packages are far more likely to go on sale than others. Finally, we have seen some evidence that suggests that products that are more popular, e.g. eggs at Easter, are the products that retailers are most likely to put on sale. To further explore the relationship between product popularity and the likelihood that the retailer puts the product on sale we use a data set from A. C. Nielsen which allows us to relate a product's market share to the probability it goes on sale.

Specifically, using the Neilsen data, we regress the probability a product goes on sale on the product's share of revenue within its category. We define a *product* as a particular brand and size of a product (e.g. 18 ounce container of Skippy Creamy peanut butter) and the probability a product goes on sale is the proportion of store weeks that particular size is on sale.[21] Similarly, the market share for a *product* is the share for that specific brand and size, calculated at the city level over the entire time period. Hence, each observation in the data set consists of a product's estimated probability of going on sale and its market share. We estimate this regression separately for each of the seven product categories in the data set (ketchup, tub margarine, stick margarine, peanut butter, sugar, facial tissue, and tuna) and for both cities (Sioux Falls, South Dakota and Springfield, Missouri). For each product, city, and both definitions of a sale (as well as definitions not reported here), we find a positive relationship between a product's market share and the likelihood it goes on sale (see table 9). Further, for Springfield, Missouri for all products but tub margarine, the result is statistically significant at conventional levels, and for Sioux Fall, South Dakota using a 10% sale definition the result is statistically significant for all products except peanut butter. Considering the very small sample sizes in the regression, these results imply that a strongly positive relationship exists.[22]

VI. Conclusion

Several recent papers have provided empirical evidence suggesting that retailer competition results in periodic price changes even when costs are unchanged. However, each of these studies provides evidence about sale behavior for a relatively small number of products from a few retail establishments. This paper attempts to broaden our understanding of these pricing dynamics by providing more systematic evidence about retail prices. Our data covers a large number of products

---

[21] Where a sale is defined as before, a temporary price decrease of a given amount followed in the next week by a similar increase.

[22] While these results are consistent with the hypothesis that more popular products are put on sale, it is also consistent with the causality running in the opposite direction; products with lower average prices have greater market shares. In any case, the empirical finding of a positive relationship between the two seems robust.

across a variety of urban areas for a ten year period. Our results suggests that a number of pricing regularities exists for all of these goods. First, for each of twenty categories of goods in our BLS sample, stores seem to have a "regular" price, and most deviations from that price are downward. Second, we find there is considerable heterogeneity in sale behavior across goods in each category; within each category of goods, the same items are regularly put on sale, while other items are rarely, if ever, put on sale. Third, the probability of a sale on an item appears to be greater when demand for that item is highest. Fourth, for the limited number of items for which we know category market shares, there is a statistically significant positive relationship between the likelihood a product is on sale, and its market share.

These latter three observations are consistent with the extension of the Lal and Matutes model presented in Section II. This analysis predicts that relatively popular items should have more frequent sales than relatively unpopular items. More generally, we view this evidence as consistent with the premise that retailers adjust retail prices over time independent of wholesale price changes.

The evidence we have presented here combined with the work of others (both empirical and theoretical) suggests that retail sales are an important component of retail price variation, and that many of the observed instances of sales are consistent with intertemporal price discrimination. Further, these results imply that different types of consumers will effectively face different prices for the products they purchase. Consumers who can inventory (alternatively, those who can wait for a "sale") will pay a lower price than those who cannot inventory (or who choose not to wait for a "sale").

These results have several implications for empirical analysis of retailing behavior. One clear implication concerns estimating demand for individual consumer products. For instance, researchers are often interested in estimating the own and cross-price elasticities between different products. To estimate demand curves, researchers need to observe changes in price that are not associated with changes in demand; i.e. movements of a supply curve. However, if the retail price changes are primarily changes in retail margins (rather than exogenous changes in retailers' costs) that are the result of intertemporal price discrimination, then the estimated demand elasticities will be mis-measured. This occurs because the relationship derived from contemporaneous price and quantity data (even using instrumental variables to control for exogenous demand changes) does not correspond to the experiment of changing price and observing the resultant change in quantity along a demand curve. Empirically, the process that causes changes in retail price also causes changes in the position of the demand curve. In particular, as the length of time since the last sale increases, the volume of purchases consumers will make at a particular "low" price increases, and hence so does the retailer's incentive to offer a low price. Correctly measuring demand curves in this type of environment requires explicitly modeling the pricing dynamics (e.g. taking into account past prices in the demand equation).

The observation that effective prices are difficult to measure and vary across individuals implies that researchers should take care when comparing average retail prices. For example, examining the effects of a change in retailing structure (e.g., a merger) on consumers could be quite difficult. The models of sale behavior imply that the effect of a merger is to increase the length of time between sales and raise the expected sale price. This implies that consumers who purchase at the normal price will not be harmed by the merger while the inventorying customers will be. In any event, for products where sales and consumer inventory behavior are important, simply comparing the average prices of a group of items (e.g., pre and post-merger) could be a relatively uninformative measure of harm. Instead, the best way for researchers to examine the effects of changes might be to examine changes in the frequency or depth of sale or changes in shelf price.

References

Banks, Jeffrey and Sridhar Moorthy (1999) "A Model of Price Promotions with Consumer Search," *International Journal of Industrial Organization*; 17, pp. 371-98.

Conlisk, John, Eitan Gerstner, and Joel Sobel (1984) "Cyclic Pricing by a Durable Goods Monopolist," *Quarterly Journal of Economics;* 99, pp. 489-505

Hosken, Daniel and David Reiffen (1999) "Pricing Behavior of Multi-Product Retailers" *Federal Trade Commission Bureau of Economics Working Paper* 225

Levy, Daniel, Mark Bergen, Shantanu Dutta, and Robert Venable (1997) "The Magnitude of Menu Costs: Direct Evidence from Large U.S. Supermarket Chains," Q*uarterly Journal of Economics*; 112, pp. 791-825

Lal, Rajiv and Carmen Matutes (1994) "Retail Pricing and Advertising Strategies," *Journal of Business*; 67, pp. 345-70.

Lal, Rajiv and Carmen Matutes (1989) "Price Competition in Multimarket Duopolies" *Rand Journal of Economics*; 20, pp. 516-37.

Lal, Rajiv and Chakravarthi Narasimhan (1996) The Inverse Relationship Between Manufacturer and Retailer Margins: A Theory," *Marketing Science*; 15, pp. 132-151

Lach, Saul and Daniel Tsiddon (1996) "Staggering and Synchronization in Price-Setting: Evidence from Multiproduct Firms," *American Economic Review;* 86, pp. 1175-96.

Pashigian, B. Peter (1988) "Demand Uncertainty and Sales: A Study of Fashion and Markdown Pricing," *American Economic Review;* 78, pp. 936-53.

___ and Brian Bowen (1991) "Why are Products Sold on Sales?: Explanations of Pricing Regularities," *Quarterly Journal of Economics*; 106, pp.1014-1038.

Pesendorfer, Martin (1997) "Retail Sales: A Study of Pricing Behavior in Super Markets" Mimeo.

Sobel, Joel (1984) "The Timing of Sales," *Review of Economic Studies*; 51, pp. 353-68.

Steiner, Robert (1973) "Does Advertising Lower Consumer Prices?" *Journal of Marketing*; 37, pp. 19-26

Varian, Hal R. (1980) "A Model of Sales", *American Economic Review*; 70, pp. 651-9.

Warner, Elizabeth J. and Robert B. Barsky (1995) "The Timing and Magnitude of Retail Store Markdowns: Evidence from Weekends and Holiday," *Quarterly Journal of Economics*; 110, pp. 321-52.

Appendix

The appendix generalizes the analysis in Lal and Matutes (1994) by considering differences in popularity across products within a category. The Lal and Matutes model features two retailers, one at each end of a Hotelling line. Consumers are located uniformly over the line, and face unit transportation costs of T. Each retailer sells the same two goods, and for both goods, all consumers value one unit of the good at H, and have no value for a second unit of that good. Because they assume the retailers' cost of the good is zero, H can be thought of more generally as the consumers' value in excess of the retailers' cost. Finally, they assume that it costs F per good to inform consumers of the prices of individual goods. Each consumer makes their decision as to which retailer(s) to visit based on the advertised prices of the two retailers, their cost of reaching the retailers, and her expectation regarding the price of any unadvertised good.

Lal and Matutes first show that consumers correctly anticipate that the price of any unadvertised good will be H. They then show that the price of any advertised good will be strictly less than H. Finally, they show that any equilibrium will feature symmetric behavior by the two retailers; they both will advertise the same good(s) and charge the same price(s) for each good. As long as H > 2T, this equilibrium will feature all consumers buying from one of the two retailers, with all consumers buying from their nearest retailer.

We extend their analysis in three ways. First, we assume retailers sell 3 goods.[23] Second, we assume that customers are not all identical in their tastes for goods in that some consumers value each good at H, while others value it at zero. In particular, $\gamma\%$ of consumers place a value of H on the first unit of good C, $\alpha\%$ of consumers place a value of H on the first unit of good A and, $\beta\%$ place a value of H on the first unit of good B, where $\beta > \alpha$. The goods are distinguished in that while the values consumers place on goods A and B are independent of whether or not they value good C at H,

---

[23]The analysis here can be generalized to n > 3 goods with appropriate reinterpretation of γ.

25

demand for products A and B are not independent. Specifically, goods A and B are substitutes in the sense that all of the consumers that derive utility from product A view the products as perfect substitutes, while $(\beta - \alpha)$ of the customers that derive utility from B do not derive any utility from consuming A. In this sense, B is more popular than A. Conditional on consuming one unit of either good, consumers place zero value on consuming another unit of either A or B. We assume that γ, α and β are the same everywhere on the Hotelling line.

The proposition we demonstrate is that putting good A, but not good B on sale can never be an equilibrium. To do so, we first derive the equilibrium to the subgame in which both retailers put A on sale. We then demonstrate in Proposition A.1 that retailers will never choose this subgame; instead it will always be more profitable to place product B on sale instead.

Lemma A.1: In the subgame in which products A and C are advertised and product B is not, the symmetric equilibrium prices will be

$$
\begin{cases}
P_B = H \\
P_A = \dfrac{H\gamma(\beta - \alpha) + (1-\gamma)T}{1 - \alpha\gamma} \\
P_C = \dfrac{H(\alpha - \beta) + (1-\alpha)T}{1 - \alpha\gamma}
\end{cases}
$$

for both retailers.[24]

---

[24]Note that in the equilibrium derived in Lemma A.1, P_C could be negative. However, most consumers will pay a positive price for the product(s) they buy, since the sum of P_C and either P_A or P_B is positive. Specifically, P_C is more likely to be negative (i.e., negative for a larger range of values for H and T) when $(\beta - \alpha)/(1-\alpha)$ is large, which is to say, when β is closer to 1. The closer β is to 1, the larger the number of customers who are buying a positively-priced bundle. Hence, the condition under which P_C is negative also implies most consumers are buying both C and another good. Moreover, P_C is not literally negative - since we have normalized the retailer's cost at zero, negative "prices" are

Proof: As Lal and Matutes show, the price of any unadvertised good will be H. To derive the prices for the other two goods, write retailer 1's profits as

$$\pi_1 = \gamma\alpha\ x_1[P_A^1 + P_C^1] + \gamma\ x_2[(1-\beta)P_C^1 + (\beta - \alpha)(P_C^1 + H)] + \alpha(1-\gamma)x_3 P_A^1$$

where x_1 defines the position of the consumer who likes both A and C and is indifferent between purchasing those goods from the two retailers (i.e., $x_1 = \frac{1}{2} + (P_A^2 + P_C^2 - P_A^1 - P_C^1)/2T$), and x_2 and x_3 similarly respectively define the position of the marginal consumer who buys both products B and C (but not A) and A only. Maximizing π_1 with respect to P_A^1 and P_C^1 yields the following first-order conditions

$$\gamma[x_1 - \frac{P_A^1 + P_C^1}{2T}] + (1-\gamma)[x_3 - \frac{P_A^1}{2T}] = 0 \qquad (1)$$

$$\alpha[x_1 - \frac{P_A^1 + P_C^1}{2T}] + (\beta - \alpha)[x_2 - \frac{P_C^1 + H}{2T}] + (1-\beta)[x_2 - \frac{P_C^1}{2T}] = 0 \qquad (2)$$

Substituting in the definitions of the x_i, and using the fact that $P_A^2 = P_A^1$ and $P_C^2 = P_C^1$ we find that equation (1) implies $P_A^1 + \gamma P_C^1 = T$. Similarly, using $P_A^2 = P_A^1$ and $P_C^2 = P_C^1$, equation (2) implies

$$T = \alpha[P_C^1 + P_A^1] + (\beta - \alpha)[H + P_C^1] + (1-\beta)P_C^1$$

and substituting $P_A^1 = T - \gamma P_C^1$, we get

---

properly interpreted as negative margins. Finally, the possibility of negative margins is not unique to our formulation, negative margins are also possible in Lal and Matutes' model.

$$T = \alpha[T - \gamma P_C^1 + P_C^1] + (\beta - \alpha)[H + P_C^1] + (1-\beta)P_C^1 \qquad (2')$$

Solving yields

$$P_C = \frac{H(\alpha - \beta) + (1-\alpha)T}{1 - \alpha\gamma}$$

Proposition A.1: Given the above assumptions, there is no perfect Nash equilibrium in which both retailers advertise product A but not product B.

Proof: Consider an equilibrium in which product A is advertised by both retailers at $P_A^1 < H$, and product C is advertised. Suppose retailer 1 deviates by advertising B at a price of P_A^1 instead of advertising A, and charges H for A. The change in retailer 1's profit consists of four components.

$$(1-\gamma)(\beta - \alpha)P_A^1 + \gamma(\beta-\alpha)\frac{P_A^1 - H}{2} + \gamma\frac{H - P_A^1}{2T}(P_C^1 + P_A^1)(\beta - \alpha) + (1-\gamma)\frac{H - P_A^1}{2T}(P_A^1)(\beta - \alpha) \qquad (3)$$

The first term is the change in profits due to sales to customers who valued neither goods A nor C, but do value B. The second term is the lower profit due to a price decrease for B charged to customers who would have bought both goods B and C from retailer 1, even at the initial prices. The third term is the profit from additional customers who would have bought products B and C from retailer 2 at the initial price (($H - P_A^1$)/2T is the number of additional customers), and the fourth term is the profit from customers located between the midpoint of the Hotelling line and retailer 2 who would have bought nothing in the initial equilibrium, but now buy product B from retailer 1. Rewriting these latter three terms as

$$(\beta - \alpha)\frac{H - P_A^1}{2T}[-\gamma T + \gamma(P_C^1 + P_A^1) + (1-\gamma)P_A^1] \qquad (4)$$

using equation (1) we can substitute $P_A{}^1 = T - \gamma \, P_C{}^1$ into this expression, to show that the term in brackets is equal to $(1-\gamma)T$, and that the expression (3) is equal to

$$(1-\gamma)(\beta-\alpha)\frac{P_A^1+H}{2}.$$

Using the results from Lemma A.1, we see that this expression is positive. That is, it is profitable for retailer 1 to deviate, implying that advertising A and C, but not B can never be an equilibrium. ∎

It is easy to see that both retailers advertising A alone is not an equilibrium either. If both retailers were only advertising A, advertising B instead of A would allow retailer 1 to retain all of the customers who would have purchased from him in the initial "equilibrium." Moreover, these customers would pay exactly the same prices as they would have in the initial equilibrium, so that retailer 1's profits from these customers are unchanged (the per-customer expected profits are $P_A{}^1 + \gamma H$). In addition, the retailer now earns these same profits from two groups of additional customers; $(\beta-\alpha)$ customers located between retailer 1 and the midpoint of the Hotelling line, and $(\beta-\alpha)$ customers located between the midpoint and the midpoint plus $(H - P_A{}^1)/T$ (i.e., those customers who are located beyond the midpoint who would receive zero surplus from retailer 2, but get some surplus from retailer 1).∎

Table 1: Description of Data Set
by Year

Year	Proportion of Observations
1988	11.4%
1989	10.0%
1990	9.6%
1991	9.9%
1992	10.1%
1993	9.2%
1994	9.3%
1995	10.3%
1996	9.8%
1997	10.4%

Table 2: Description of Data Set

By Product

Product	Number of Price Series	Number of Observations
Baby Food	299	6579
Bananas	1142	26284
Canned Soup	1310	26480
Cereal	1631	26603
Cheese	1233	27183
Snacks	1288	21654
Cola Drinks	1116	19343
Cookies	750	14125
Crackers	311	6982
Eggs	905	27915
Frozen Dinners	561	7561
Frozen Orange Juice	491	13703
Ground Beef	909	27551
Hotdogs	471	9594
Lettuce	672	25687
Margarine	477	11826
Paper Products	620	7018
Peanut Butter	342	9188
Soap and Detergents	820	10158
White Bread	1043	24663
Total	16391	350097

Table3: Descriptive of Data Set

by Region

Region	Number of Price Series	Number of Observations
Atlanta	361	6547
Boston	570	11022
Buffalo	317	5866
Chicago	1765	40019
Cleveland	492	9730
Dallas	536	10657
Dayton	289	6733
Denver	341	6231
Detroit	1069	21404
El Paso	323	7312
Greater Los Angeles	557	15682
Jacksonville	297	7118
Kansas City	374	6033
Los Angeles	1694	35487
Miami	387	7116
Minneapolis	337	6379
New Orleans	375	6812
Suburbs of New York City	685	17816
Philadelphia	830	17270
Portland	289	5565
Richmond	385	8102
St. Louis	654	13530

San Diego	331	5556
San Francisco	947	25186
Scranton	335	6752
Seattle	355	6566
Syracuse	311	8577
Tampa	280	5515
Tucson	369	7658
Washington, D.C.	536	11856
Total	16391	350097

Table 4: Sample Description:
Frequency Distribution of Length of Time Series

	Less than 1 year	1 to 2 years	2 to 3 years	3 to 4 years	4 to 5 years	5 years or more
All Products	37.8%	24.4%	15.7%	10.1%	8.8%	3.2%
Baby Food	44.1%	17.4%	16.1%	11.0%	7.4%	4.0%
Bananas	23.6%	28.4%	26.4%	21.5%	0.1%	0%
Canned Soup	37.3%	30.5%	12.7%	9.1%	7.9%	2.5%
Cereal	51.5%	24.5%	10.1%	7.2%	5.2%	1.5%
Cheese	37.0%	23.1%	16.4%	8.7%	11.3%	3.5%
Snacks	45.3%	28.3%	12.8%	8.4%	4.7%	0.5%
Cola Drinks	40.9%	25.7%	21.1%	10.8%	1.5%	0%
Cookies	43.9%	24.2%	15.1%	6.5%	7.8%	2.5%
Crackers	31.2%	28.6%	18.0%	9.3%	10.6%	2.3%
Eggs	19.0%	23.2%	16.3%	13.2%	19.5%	8.8%
Frozen Dinners	56.7%	24.4%	11.8%	4.8%	2.1%	0.2%
Frozen Orange Juice	26.5%	20.3%	16.7%	14.5%	15.1%	6.9%
Ground Beef	19.0%	23.4%	17.8%	13.5%	18.3%	8.0%
Hotdogs	40.3%	22.5%	18.1%	8.7%	8.9%	1.5%
Lettuce	6.8%	17.9%	19.1%	15.4%	27.7%	13.1%
Margarine	32.1%	24.3%	14.2%	9.3%	15.9%	4.2%
Paper Products	64.4%	22.2%	9.4%	2.0%	0.9%	0.6%
Peanut Butter	28.4%	16.0%	22.6%	13.1%	13.2%	6.7%
Soap and Detergents	61.0%	23.6%	9.4%	2.2%	3.1%	0.6%
White Bread	34.6%	21.8%	17.4%	10.6%	11.8%	3.8%

Table 5: Summary of Frequency Distributions of

How Often Price Quotes are at Their Modal Value

Product	Proportion of Time Series at Modal Price less than or equal to 25% of Time	Proportion of Time Series at Modal Price less than 50% of Time	Proportion of Time Series at Modal Price more than 75% of Time	Annual Price Series
Baby Food	0.4%	12.7%	47.3%	790
Bananas	17.6%	42.8%	17.5%	3788
Canned Soup	2.1%	19.7%	39.3%	3570
Cereal	3.2%	21.5%	39.9%	3709
Cheese	6.1%	28.7%	37.5%	3568
Snacks	2.0%	14.1%	50.6%	3074
Cola Drinks	10.3%	34.7%	36.2%	2855
Cookies	4.0%	19.2%	48.6%	1917
Crackers	4.9%	26.3%	35.7%	892
Eggs	48.4%	75.7%	11.1%	4465
Frozen Dinners	1.4%	18.5%	46.0%	1247
Frozen Orange Juice	8.5%	35.0%	24.9%	1672
Ground Beef	7.8%	35.6%	28.2%	3240
Hot Dogs	7.2%	31.9%	36.7%	1274
Lettuce	93.0%	96.6%	1.7%	12213
Margarine	7.4%	31.5%	34.8%	1461
Paper Products	4.3%	19.9%	41.5%	1552

Peanut Butter	5.1%	27.1%	34.3%	1099
Soap and Detergent	4.1%	18.0%	42.5%	2194
White Bread	2.9%	21.5%	56.9%	3063

Table 6: Percentage of Prices Above and Below the Annual Modal Price By Product

	Percentage Above Mode[i]	Percentage Below Mode[i]	Z-Statistic[ii] (P value)
Baby Food	9.5 (592)	16.6 (1032)	3.95 (.0000)
Bananas	14.0 (3371)	28.2 (6791)	15.88 (.0000)
Canned Soup	10.5 (2615)	20.3 (5043)	10.81 (.0000)
Cereal	11.6 (2885)	20.3 (5038)	9.85 (.0000)
Cheese	12.8 (3238)	19.7 (4986)	8.15 (.0000)
Snacks	7.0 (1453)	17.2 (3581)	9.40 (.0000)
Cola Drinks	10.5 (1872)	23.5 (4184)	11.80 (.0000)
Cookies	7.8 (1049)	18.6 (2491)	8.09 (.0000)
Crackers	7.8 (516)	25.7 (1699)	8.66 (.0000)
Eggs	25.6 (5795)	32.4 (7346)	8.55 (.0000)
Frozen Dinners	7.8 (552)	21.6 (1531)	7.24 (.0000)

Frozen Orange Juice	12.3 (1560)	27.5 (3479)	11.86 (0000)
Ground Beef	11.8 (2996)	25.6 (6480)	15.22 (0000)
Hotdogs	10.2 (908)	24.3 (2170)	8.92 (0000)
Lettuce	18.2 (4206)	65.0 (15007)	53.84 (0000)
Margarine	11.1 (1222)	23.4 (2576)	8.95 (0000)
Paper Products	9.2 (602)	22.3 (1454)	6.94 (0000)
Peanut Butter	11.5 (984)	22.2 (1904)	7.03 (0000)
Soap and Detergents	8.7 (832)	20.8 (1996)	7.79 (0000)
White Bread	10.6 (2462)	18.0 (4183)	8.11 (0000)

i Number of observations in parentheses.

ii P-Values in parentheses.

Table 7 - Percent of Price Series Experiencing at Least One Sale in the Second Year of the Sample, Conditional on Whether there is a Sale within the First Year

Panel a - sale = 10% reduction

Product	Conditional on at least one sale within the First Year (number of price series)	Conditional on no Sale within the First Year (number of price series)	Z-Statistic (p-value)
Baby Food	26.7% (15)	3.7% (82)	3.17 (.0016)
Bananas	84.0% (401)	52.9% (87)	6.41 (0)
Canned Soup	51.8% (110)	17.4% (265)	6.81 (0)
Cereal	53.2% (77)	22.0% (259)	5.29 (0)
Cheese	56.1% (139)	21.0% (257)	7.07 (0)
Snacks	68.5% (124)	25.8% (151)	7.08 (0)
Cola Drinks	72.0% (157)	25.4% (122)	7.72 (0)
Cookies	66.7% (63)	20.0% (115)	6.18 (0)
Crackers	84.9% (53)	25.5% (51)	6.10 (0)

Eggs	63.5% (244)	38.5% (218)	5.37 (0)
Frozen Dinners	60.9% (46)	34.2% (38)	2.43 (.015)
Frozen Orange Juice	64.6% (113)	36.4% (118)	4.28 (0)
Ground Beef	70.3% (246)	36.1% (216)	7.37 (0)
Hot Dogs	65.1% (83)	37.5% (56)	3.20 (.0014)
Lettuce	96.1% (417)	70.0% (40)	6.59 (0)
Margarine	66.2% (74)	32.1% (109)	4.54 (0)
Paper Products	76.5% (17)	32.3% (31)	2.93 (.0034)
Peanut Butter	49.0% (51)	17.4% (109)	4.17 (0)
Soap and Detergent	64.5% (31)	21.2% (33)	3.51 (.0004)
White Bread	60.9% (151)	15.0% (233)	9.34 (0)

Panel b - sale = 20% reduction

Product	Conditional on at least one Sale within the First Year (number of price series)	Conditional on no Sale within the First Year (number of price series)	Z-Statistic (p-value)
Baby Food	50.0% (2)	3.2% (7)	3.29 (0.0012)
Bananas	72.4% (333)	49.0% (155)	5.03 (0)
Canned Soup	32.0% (50)	10.8% (325)	4.08 (0)
Cereal	54.5% (44)	14.7% (292)	6.16 (0)
Cheese	44.0% (75)	13.1% (321)	6.15 (0)
Snacks	56.8% (88)	23.0% (187)	5.53 (0)
Cola Drinks	52.8% (108)	17.5% (171)	6.19 (0)
Cookies	44.8% (29)	13.4% (149)	3.98 (0)
Crackers	60.0% (35)	25.0% (64)	3.57 (.0004)

Eggs	49.6% (121)	15.5% (341)	7.48 (0)
Frozen Dinners	60.0% (35)	16.3% (49)	4.15 (0)
Frozen Orange Juice	56.5% (85)	24.7% (146)	4.85 (0)
Ground Beef	54.6% (130)	21.1% (332)	7.04 (0)
Hot Dogs	52.7% (55)	32.1% (84)	2.42 (.0156)
Lettuce	83.0% (358)	71.7% (99)	2.50 (.0124)
Margarine	54.8% (42)	18.4% (141)	4.67 (0)
Paper Products	50.0% (6)	21.4% (42)	1.51 (0.131)
Peanut Butter	28.6% (21)	5.8% (139)	3.45 (.0006)
Soap and Detergent	42.9% (14)	10.0% (50)	2.88 (.004)
White Bread	44.1% (102)	12.1% (282)	6.86 (0)

Table 8: Probability of Sale for Various /

Products in Relatively High and Low Periods of Demand

Panel a - Sale = 10% reduction

Product	Probability of Sale in High Demand Period	Probability of Sale in Low Demand Period	Z-Statistic for difference in Probability
Ground Beef	0.0899	0.0675	3.99
Hot Dogs	0.1022	0.0730	2.93
Eggs	0.1342	0.0623	4.49
Canned Soup	0.0404	0.0264	6.14
Peanut Butter	0.0474	0.0336	2.64

Panel b - Sale = 20% reduction

Product	Probability of Sale in High Demand Period	Probability of Sale in Low Demand Period	Z-Statistic for difference in Probability
Ground Beef	0.04562	0.03039	3.95
Hot Dogs	0.06080	0.04432	2.10
Eggs	0.03896	0.02536	1.30
Canned Soup	0.01850	0.01171	4.14
Peanut Butter	0.02306	0.01119	3.68

Table 9 - RELATIONSHIP BETWEEN PROBABILITY OF A SALE ON A PRODUCT AND ITS CATEGORY MARKET SHARE

Panel a: Sioux Falls, Sale =10 %

Product	Intercept		Market Share		P Value for Slope Coef.	R-squared	Obs.
	Estimate	Error	Estimate	Error			
Ketchup	0.0023	0.0038	0.0022	0.0004	0.0001	0.6843	15
Margarine -	0.0161	0.0096	0.0047	0.0009	0.0003	0.7073	13
Margarine -	-0.0045	0.0044	0.0045	0.0007	0.0001	0.6673	20
Peanut Butter	0.0142	0.0074	0.0029	0.0020	0.1681	0.0692	29
Sugar	0.0067	0.0077	0.0050	0.0018	0.0129	0.3120	19
Tissue	0.0180	0.0076	0.0050	0.0019	0.0177	0.2299	24
Tuna	0.020	0.012	0.002	0.001	0.0333	0.350	13

Table 9 - (con't)

Panel b: Springfield, Sale =10 %

Product	Intercept		Market Share		P Value for	R-squared	Obs.
	Estimate	Error	Estimate	Error	Slope Coef.		
Ketchup	-0.0033	0.0029	0.0026	0.0004	0.0001	0.7003	19
Margarine -	-0.0014	0.0029	0.0036	0.0003	0.0001	0.8919	17
Margarine - Tubs	0.0037	0.0023	0.0002	0.0006	0.7340	0.0040	31
Peanut Butter	-0.0008	0.0028	0.0035	0.0006	0.0001	0.6289	24
Sugar	0.0091	0.0113	0.0043	0.0016	0.0246	0.4114	12
Tissue	0.0141	0.0081	0.0048	0.0018	0.0145	0.2639	22
Tuna	0.0080	0.0043	0.0023	0.0003	0.0001	0.7624	17

Table 9 - (con't)

Panel c: Sioux Falls, Sale = 20 %

Product	Intercept		Market Share		P Value for Slope Coef.	R-squared	Obs.
	Estimate	Error	Estimate	Error			
Ketchup	0.0006	0.0032	0.0012	0.0003	0.0052	0.4637	15
Margarine -	0.0156	0.0080	0.0021	0.0008	0.0186	0.4091	13
Margarine - Tubs	-0.0069	0.0022	0.0032	0.0004	0.0001	0.8075	20
Peanut Butter	0.0047	0.0029	0.0004	0.0008	0.6252	0.0090	29
Sugar	0.0057	0.0030	0.0001	0.0007	0.8595	0.0019	19
Tissue	0.0100	0.0049	0.0017	0.0012	0.1943	0.0753	24
Tuna	0.0096	0.0071	0.0012	0.0005	0.0209	0.3973	13

Table 9 - (con't)

Panel d: Springfield, Sale = 20 %

Product	Intercept		Market Share		P Value for Slope Coef.	R-squared	Obs.
	Estimate	Error	Estimate	Error			
Ketchup	-0.0022	0.0017	0.0016	0.0002	0.0001	0.7254	19
Margarine -	-0.0046	0.0020	0.0031	0.0002	0.0001	0.9308	17
Margarine -	0.0014	0.0016	0.0002	0.0004	0.6909	0.0055	31
Peanut Butter	-0.0018	0.0021	0.0025	0.0004	0.0001	0.5974	24
Sugar	0.0080	0.0107	0.0042	0.0015	0.0197	0.0197	12
Tissue	0.0068	0.0053	0.0034	0.0012	0.0032	0.3598	22
Tuna	0.0070	0.0037	0.0019	0.0003	0.0001	0.7497	17